Do You See Me?

BECKY BLACKMON

Publishing Designs, Inc.
P.O. Box 3241
Huntsville, Alabama 35810

Cover and page design: CrosslinCreative.net
Editors: Peggy Coulter and Debra G. Wright

Publisher's Cataloging-in-Publication Data

Blackmon, Becky 1948—

Do You See Me? / Becky Blackmon

102 pp.

10 chapters and study questions

1. Lesser-Known Old Testament Bible Women. 2. Interactive Bible Study. 3. Culture. Grief. Courage. Choices.

I. Title.

ISBN 978-1-945127-37-3

248.8

DEDICATION

This book is lovingly dedicated to all the Pearl Seekers who strive to know our God.

Again, the kingdom of heaven is like a merchant seeking fine pearls, and upon finding one pearl of great value, he went and sold all that he had and bought it.

—Matthew 13:45–46

CONTENTS

Foreword. 7

Introduction 9

Wading in the Water: *"Gentile Women, Jewish Men"*. 11
1 Bithia, the Courageous Egyptian 13

Wading in the Water: *"A Head for Business"* 19
2 Achsah, the Intelligent and Cherished Daughter. 21

Wading in the Water: *"Girls, Come and Help"* 27
3 The Amazing Daughters of Shallum 29

Wading in the Water: *"Women with No Voice but Their Own"*. . . . 37
4 The Courageous and Bold Daughters of Zelophehad. 39

Wading in the Water: *"The Littlest Missionary"*. 45
5 Slave Girl with a Heart of Gold. 47

Wading in the Water: *"God Has a Plan"* 53
6 Don't Mess with Jael: A Woman's Mighty Arm. 57

Wading in the Water: *"Weeping over Grown Children"* 65
7 Rizpah: One Tragic Heartbroken Mother! 67

Wading in the Water: *"God's Got a Hedge"* 75
8 Shiphrah and Puah: Saviors of a Nation 77

Wading in the Water: *"The Road Not Taken"* 83
9 Orpah, Think Again! 85

Wading in the Water: *"I Have a Question!"* 91
10 The Queen of Sheba: The Pearl Seeker 93

A Final Word. 99

PREFACE

Approximately 2,400 years ago, God uttered these poignant words to the weeping prophet Jeremiah:

> *My people are foolish,*
> *They have not known Me.*
> *They are silly children,*
> *And they have no understanding.*
> *They are wise to do evil,*
> *But to do good they have no knowledge.*

Could there be any sadder verse in the entire Bible than this one in Jeremiah 4:22 (NKJV)? Could there be any sadder words than these from the mouth of our God? Our Father, the creator of the universe, poured out His heart to Jeremiah and bemoaned the lost condition of His family, Israel. Immoral, idol-worshiping, child-sacrificing, and rebellious were God's sons and daughters—a family chosen from before the earth was formed—and yet doomed for Babylonian captivity and death.

Fast forward to the present. Jeremiah's words from God still strike sorrow in our hearts! Why? Because they can still be applied to many Christians today—God's sons and daughters—who are senseless children and fools, children who do not know their Father.

We expect this kind of behavior from the world, but not from God's people! Consider the goodness of God; consider His blessings and provisions for the entire world. On top of all this, ponder His offer of salvation and His love in sending His Son to die for every single one of us.

History repeats itself as some of God's children once again do not know God. They don't know who He is because they don't read His Word. They have no knowledge of the Father, the Savior, or the Holy Spirit because they have no desire to know. And the saddest part of all is that many Christians have no desire to obey His Word. Oh, they want to obey the gospel and be saved, but somewhere along the line many lose interest in listening to the Father and begin walking with Satan, listening to his lies. They make the decision to serve one master—and leave the other.

Where do you stand in this, my Christian friend? What is your relationship with the Father? Do you care about His Word and try to understand it? Do you know how to do good, or not?

This book has been written to help you find God, understand His nature, and receive His love. Take your time; look up the passages; get out your maps and find the places where God's people lived. The moment has come; it is time to learn.

I implore you: Will you turn your life around? Will you get into the Word and change your life? Remember, only you can change your soul's destiny.

Someone has said, "Many will miss heaven by eighteen inches, the distance from their head to their heart. They know about Christ, but do not know Him. You can be religious but lost. You can have the Bible in your head but not have Christ in your heart."

The ancient haunting words from the Lord echo in our ears every day: "My people are fools; they do not know Me."

My prayer for you and me is this: "Please, Lord, don't let us be fools. Please let us know You."

INTRODUCTION
STOP, LOOK, AND READ AGAIN!

Have you ever been reading God's marvelous Word and suddenly stumble upon an unusual character or an extraordinary event that seems to be hidden away among the verses? Bells and whistles go off in your head—ding, ding, ding! Perhaps it is only one verse that describes an event or person, but there it lies, and the thing is you may have read through the Bible year after year and never noticed it.

So what do you do? You stop dead in your tracks. You screech to a grinding halt and back up . . . and read that verse again. And again. And again. And there it is—a single moment for you that God has been sharing with the world for several thousand years, and you have never seen it.

Personally, I love it when this happens to me. I call these events "zingers," and every time I discover one, my heart soars! A zinger has the power to completely turn me around and stop my world. I find it frequently popping up in my brain to the extent that I want to talk about it wherever I go. And that is exactly what is happening right now.

I want to share some of these unique zingers with the world. Now you have to understand that most of these biblical people or events might take up only one verse. Sometimes the outstanding individual is unnamed. But what the true Bible student must do is pause, dig, research, and learn.

In the lessons ahead, please read each "Wading in the Water" preview to give you an idea of the chapter contents. Read the biblical verses out loud. Get out your maps and timelines. Study the locations presented. Read the commentary notes at the end of each lesson— you will even find some answers there. And, above all, ask the questions that spring up from personal pondering. It is possible that you might even identify with the main character!

Do you know what will happen after that? You will grow. Your faith will grow. You may not have all the answers in a particular event, and that's just fine. However, you will stand amazed at what God has done, not only in your own life but also in the life of the character you have just discovered! Your realization of who God is and the infinite greatness of His power will astound you in every possible way. Oh, the lessons our Father is trying to teach you and me—if only we would open His Book.

I hope and pray that you are a daily Bible reader. If you are, you know how some books in the Bible are extra challenging, especially those from the Old Testament. These books may be filled with numbers and strategic placements of the twelve tribes along with descriptions of the tabernacle and the temple. Whatever you do, do not stop reading! Keep on. Your brain is absorbing more than you think it is! An astonishing thing happens as you read the Bible year in and year out: you begin to understand what God is saying and trying to describe to you. Your brain is assembling the information and comprehending the picture the Master Artist is drawing. On top of that, you just might find a hidden zinger—I imagine this as a tone, ding, ding, ding—in one of those difficult passages. It's like God is waiting for us to uncover His messages. But please remember one thing: All our questions are not answered. We can only wonder about the details. That's okay.

Discussions will ensue in these chapters, but *no arguing allowed!* Just try to keep an open mind and realize there are some references where we do not have the final answer. We can pray for patience and understanding and then wait.

You and I are on a treasure hunt when we open the Bible, so let's see what treasures we can find. Travel with me, my Christian family, and let's discover what the Father wants all His children to see in the fascinating women and events of only a few verses. It's time to learn!

WADING IN THE WATER

GENTILE WOMEN, JEWISH MEN

How easy is it to be married to a person from another culture? Think of the obstacles that must be overcome: language, customs, manners, etc. And often it's complicated because of religion. Most married couples experience the challenges of marital bliss—finances, raising children, and education, to name a few. In addition, often there's confusion and conflict because of a socioeconomic society where one may not be accepted. Then exclusion is experienced on many levels. Racism is nothing new.

Before you wade into this chapter, think of a few Gentile women who married Jewish men. Who comes to mind?

The Old Testament gives us accounts of Gentiles and Hebrews intermarrying. We are mindful of Ruth and Orpah, Gentile women who married Jewish men. And the New Testament mentions Eunice, a Jewess who had married a Greek. But we must remember that our God loves all His creation.

When I read the story of Ruth, I am reminded of God's love in caring for a Gentile woman from the land of Moab. Many call the story of Ruth and Boaz a love story, and it surely is. But most of all it is a remarkable story of conversion. Ruth left her father's home and native land to stay with her husband's family and ancestors and embrace their God. God had a plan for Ruth and Boaz to find one another, love one another, and establish a bloodline from which the Messiah would come. Their love story truly is remarkable.

So let's put on our thinking caps and imagine what life would have been like for a lesser-known Gentile—a beautiful princess who left her father's palace to cross the Red Sea in that cataclysmic event of the Exodus. Here God gives us a Jewish man and an Egyptian woman who found one another during turbulent times. Surely God had a plan for this couple and for this woman who left the idols of Egypt and embraced Yahweh.

May I introduce to you, Bithia, the convert.

CHAPTER
1

Bithia, The Courageous Egyptian

Scripture: 1 Chronicles 4:17–18
Song: "Give Me the Bible"

Today you are going to meet a very brave woman. She is a hidden treasure that I have lately discovered in my daily Bible reading. I feel so ashamed at never seeing her before . . . but then, my God is so merciful to me. And I know He is to you. That's just the way He is. I found her name tucked away among all the men's names from the tribe of Judah.

First Chronicles begins with Adam. If you have a study Bible, you can perhaps find a timeline. Here God starts at the beginning of time and names the people and the events up to the time of David, the shepherd king.

Use the maps in your Bible to find Israel and Egypt. Find Jerusalem, then locate the Sea of Galilee and the Dead Sea. Get familiar with Palestine. You might prefer online maps. Here is an example: https://thebiblesays.com/wp-content/uploads/2018/09/oldtestamentmap.jpg.

Carefully read 1 Chronicles 4:17–18. Find the Jewish man named Mered in verse 17. Focus on the woman Bithia, a wife of Mered. Let's read about her and talk about what we know or think we know.

> The sons of Ezrah *were* Jether, Mered, Epher and Jalon.
> (And these are the sons of Bithia the daughter of Pha-
> raoh, whom Mered took) and she conceived and bore Mir-
> iam, Shammai and Ishbah the father of Eshtemoa. His
> Jewish wife bore Jered the father of Gedor, and Heber
> the father of Soco, and Jekuthiel the father of Zanoah
> (1 Chron. 4:17–18).

Who is this woman? We see she is an Egyptian princess, a daughter of Pharaoh. But she does not have an Egyptian name, so read your
notes in your Bible or research online to find out what her name means.
Write the meaning here. _____

I hope questions are popping into your head right now. How
did it happen that this princess traveled into the wilderness with
the Israelites as they fled from the Egyptians? Remember Exodus
12:35–38 tells us of a "mixed multitude" that went with the Jews.
Pause and think about it.

Let's see the information God has given us in Exodus 12:37–38.

> Now the sons of Israel journeyed from Rameses to Suc-
> coth, about six hundred thousand men on foot, aside from
> children. A mixed multitude also went up with them, along
> with flocks and herds, a very large number of livestock.

TIME FOR A CLOSER LOOK

Research to find a date for the exodus of the Israelites from Egypt.

1. Where does all this take place?

_____

_____

_____

2. Who is our main character, and where is she from?

_____

_____

_____

3. How does she wind up in 1 Chronicles?

_____

_____

_____

4. Who is her husband?

_____

5. Read 1 Chronicles 4:18 and see that Mered had a _____ wife, as well as Bithia.

6. Write our character's name and give the meaning, using appropriate resource material.

_____

_____

_____

_____

7. How might the Egyptian woman and the Jewish man have met?

_____

_____

_____

8. List some possible marital conflicts that Bithia and Mered might have experienced because of their different ethnic backgrounds.

_____

_____

_____

_____

_____

_____

9. Read Exodus 12:35–38 and tell how the Jews plundered the Egyptians. Who had told the Jews to ask the Egyptians for gold, silver, and clothing?

WHAT OTHERS HAVE SAID

Burton Coffman: [In Exodus 2 concerning the one who drew Moses from the Nile]—We cannot identify this daughter of Pharaoh. Josephus called her Thermutis, and Eusebius called her Merris. Unger suggested that her name might have been Hatshepsut, the only woman known to have become a Pharaoh. But until ancient Egyptian history is much more than the patchwork of guesses that it is today, the certain identification is impossible.[1]

Albert Barnes: Mered, it would seem, had two wives, Bithiah [Bithia], an Egyptian woman, and a Jewish wife whose name is not given. If Mered was a chief of rank, Bithiah may have been married to him with the consent of her father, for the Egyptian kings often gave their daughters in marriage to foreigners. Or she may have elected to forsake her countrymen and cleave to a Jewish husband, becoming a convert to his religion. Her name, Bithiah, "daughter of Yahweh," is like that of a convert.[2]

---

1 Burton Coffman, *Coffman's Commentaries on the Bible*, Exodus 2:5–6, accessed Jan. 11, 2024. https://www.studylight.org/commentaries/eng/bcc/exodus-2.html.

2 Albert Barnes, *Barnes' Notes on the Whole Bible*, 1 Chronicles 4:18, accessed Jan. 11, 2024. https://www.studylight.org/commentaries/eng/bnb/1-chronicles-4.html.

BOTTOM L|NE

What is God trying to tell us in revealing her story? Why do you think God allows us to meet her?

PRAYER

Our Father, we praise Your name today and always. Thank You for Your marvelous Word and the wonderful accounts of Your family. We thank You for Bithia and for her love and desire to be one of Your daughters even though she had a different upbringing from the people around her. Please help us always to look for Your truth and Your guidance. Please give us the courage to see what is right, do what is right in Your sight, and stand up for You. We love You. In Jesus' name, Amen.

WADING IN THE WATER

A HEAD FOR BUSINESS

Having a head for business and money matters is a quality highly esteemed in the world today. We raise our sons to pursue a good education and find a vocation that will be challenging and profitable. We do the same thing with our daughters. In America the sky is the limit for any person climbing the ladder of success.

We admire those who achieve their goals by means of hard work and unrelenting ideals of honesty and fairness. The television networks run regular stories of young and old entrepreneurs who have found that the secrets of success are kindness and second-mile service.

On the other hand, we are aware of the power of money and the greed factor. Paul wrote to a young Timothy,

> For the love of money is a root of all sorts of evil, and some by longing for it have wandered away from the faith and pierced themselves with many griefs (1 Tim. 6:10).

How many times have we seen a public figure rise to power only to fall to the lowest of lows because of a Ponzi scheme or a plan to bilk millions from innocent individuals? The desire for money has ruined many a man and woman. "The deceitfulness of riches" are words that come to mind from the parable of the sower in Mark 4:19.

However, there are those who have a head for business and know how to serve the customer. Think of the talented men and women who can design and sew fabulous dresses, purses, and scarves. "These designers can make a killing," we are known to say. Remember the "Worthy Woman" of Proverbs 31? God has this to say about her: "She makes linen garments and sells them, and supplies belts to the tradesmen" (Prov. 31:24). She must have been quite an accomplished woman!

Another woman mentioned in the Old Testament who had a head for business and acted upon it is Achsah. Some think she was greedy. Some think she was smart. Let's meet her and see what we think.

CHAPTER 2

Achsah, The Intelligent And Cherished Daughter

Scripture: Joshua 15:16–19; 1 Chronicles 2:48–49

Song: "I Know the Lord Will Find a Way for Me"

In today's class we will meet a woman of many talents. Once again, she popped up in one of my daily Bible readings. As usual, I had not seen her for years. I was not thinking as I was reading, and that is a bad habit of mine. God mentions her in two different places in the Old Testament, and her story is intriguing.

I call Achsah the smart cookie! Because she is! Achsah hails from a very prominent Israelite family and wilderness hero. I am talking about that famous spy from the tribe of Judah, Caleb. Achsah makes a bold request of her father. Her request does not seem to faze Caleb, and he grants her petition. Let's also note that obtaining land and water rights can have monetary benefits.

Those of us who have had a good relationship with our fathers can easily relate the instances of climbing up on good ol' Dad's lap and asking him a favor. (How many times can you remember doing that?) Achsah must have put a lot of thought into this request. What do you think?

One further thought: She must have been special because God does not always mention the names of daughters in the Bible.

No more procrastination—let's jump into the Word and learn about a very smart and beloved daughter of Israel.

> And Caleb said, "The one who attacks Kiriath-sepher and captures it, I will give him Achsah my daughter as a wife." Othniel the son of Kenaz, the brother of Caleb, captured it; so he gave him Achsah his daughter as a wife. It came about that when she came to him, she persuaded him to ask her father for a field. So she alighted from the donkey, and Caleb said to her, "What do you want?" Then she said, "Give me a blessing; since you have given me the land of the Negev, give me also springs of water." So he gave her the upper springs and the lower springs (Josh. 15:16–19).
>
> Maacah, Caleb's concubine, bore Sheber and Tirhanah. She also bore Shaaph the father of Madmannah, Sheva the father of Machbena and the father of Gibea; and the daughter of Caleb *was* Achsah (1 Chron. 2:48–49).

TIME FOR A CLOSER LOOK

1. What is an approximate date of Achsah's story?

2. Where does this account take place?

3. Who was Achsah's famous father? To what tribe did he and Achsah's husband belong?

4. Who won Achsah's hand in marriage? What did he have to accomplish in order to marry her?

5. What did Achsah want him to do in Joshua 15:18?

6. What had evidently been her dowry (Josh. 15:19)? Describe this gift—pros and cons.

7. Who in this story is the one who actually asked for water rights?

8. What distinction does Othniel have in the Old Testament?

9. How does owning these rights benefit Achsah and her descendants?

10. Would there even be possible monetary benefits? How?

WHAT OTHERS HAVE SAID

Matthew Henry: He gave her a south land, Joshua 15:19. Land indeed, but a south land, dry, and apt to be parched. She obtained more upon her request; she would have had her husband to ask for a field, probably some particular field . . . which belonged to Caleb's lot, and joined to that south land which he had settled upon his daughter at marriage. She thought her husband had the best interest in her father, who, no doubt, was extremely pleased with his late glorious achievement, but he thought it was more proper for her to ask, and she would be more likely to prevail; . . . and she managed the undertaking with great address. . . . She calls it a blessing, because it would add much to the comfort of her settlement; and she was sure that, since she married not only with her father's consent, but in obedience to his command, he would not deny her his blessing. . . . She asks only for the water, without which the ground she had would be of little use either for tillage or pasture, but she means the field in which the springs of water were. The modesty and reasonableness of her quest gave it a great advantage. Earth without water would be like a tree without sap, or the body of an animal without blood; therefore, when God gathered the waters into one place, he wisely and graciously left some in every place, that the earth might be enriched for the service of man. . . . Achsah gained her point. Her father gave her what she asked, and perhaps more, for he gave her the upper springs and the nether springs, two fields so called from the springs that were in them, as we commonly distinguish between the higher field and the lower field.[1]

John Calvin: Although we may conjecture that the damsel Achsah was of excellent morals and well brought up, as marriage with her had been held forth as the special reward of victory, yet perverse cupidity on her part is here disclosed. She knew that by the divine law women were specially excluded from hereditary lands, but she nevertheless

---

1 Matthew Henry, *Henry's Complete Commentary on the Bible*, Joshua 15:13–19, accessed Jan. 11, 2024. https://www.studylight.org/commentaries/eng/mhm/joshua-15.html.

covets the possession of them, and stimulates her husband by unjust expostulation. . . .

But a greater degree of intemperance is displayed when she acquires additional boldness from the facility of her husband and the indulgence of her father. Not contented with the field given to her, she demands for herself a well-watered district. And thus it is when a person has once overleaped the bounds of rectitude and honesty, the fault is forthwith followed up by impudence. Moreover, her father in refusing her nothing gives proof of his singular affection for her. . . . It is more simple, however, to suppose that she placed herself at her father's feet with the view of accosting him as a suppliant. Be this as it may, by her craft and flattery she gained his consent, and in so far diminished the portion of her brothers.[2]

BOTTOM LINE

God sees to it that we read about Achsah twice in the Bible. What do you think the Lord wants us to see? What would you have done if you had been Achsah?

_____

_____

_____

_____

_____

_____

_____

_____

_____

_____

---

2 John Calvin, *Calvin's Commentary on the Bible,* Joshua 15:18, accessed Jan. 11, 2024. https://www.studylight.org/commentaries/eng/cal/joshua-15.html.

PRAYER

We thank You, our Father, for Your marvelous love and mercy. Thank You for telling us about You and the accounts of Your people. Please help us to learn from Achsah and see her kindnesses her father bestowed upon her. Lord, please help us parents to diligently teach our children about You. And please help us to be a blessing in our children's lives. Please help us as parents to show them Your way home. In Jesus' name, Amen.

WADING IN THE WATER

GIRLS, COME AND HELP!

I learned a great deal from watching my parents. From the time I was a young girl, I can remember seeing my parents sitting in the living room reading their Bibles aloud together. It was a daily occurrence. They would sit there, read, and then discuss what they had just read. They asked a lot of questions! And that is what we must do when reading this precious Book. Stopping and pausing and studying passages help us to grow and strengthen our faith.

Reading the Bible was part of my parents' daily walk with God, and they never would have dreamed of neglecting it. They stressed the importance of God's Word to us children, surrounded us with many Bibles, and taught us to be daily Bible readers from an early age. What a marvelous gift that has been to me! How thankful I am for godly parents who not only taught me the importance of reading God's Word, but who also demonstrated it personally.

The Fowler home was noisy, fun, spiritual, and busy. My parents both had a very strong work ethic and somehow had the notion that their children should learn the "joy" of chores. And somehow, we learned it—mostly through Mom teaching us the pride of a job well done and the reward called an allowance.

My brother Tom was the eldest of us three children—Tom, Judy, and me. When Tom left for college, things changed. Dad had lost his helper. Suddenly it seemed that Dad needed our (the girls') assistance. Judy and I were on call. We helped Dad because he was always fixing something that was broken. I learned how to start a car by popping the clutch as Dad pushed it down a hill, and I even found myself trotting along with Dad when hunting for rabbits and gophers in farmers' fields. I knew how to handle a gun from an early age, but now Dad was trying to teach me the joy of the hunt. (No, I never learned it—and I'm sure the animals were most grateful.)

Mom and Dad loved to go camping. They bought several types of campers through the years. Their last model was an Apache, a pop-up camper they purchased when I was in college. We would load the car, hitch the camper up, and head off to here, there, and yon. Upon finding our camping spot, Dad would carefully back the Apache in and then holler, "Becky, come and help." Out of the car I climbed (sometimes unwillingly) to help Dad chock the wheels, unhitch and level the camper, and unpack the gear. Judy usually had to help Mom. It was a lot of work—but it was also making memories.

I tell you these things because every time I read the book of Nehemiah, I meet a father and his daughters who make me think of my home and my family. For some reason, I can just hear Shallum of chapter 3 hollering, "Girls, come and help. We are going to build a wall!" And of course, they came running.

Let us meet the amazing daughters of Shallum.

CHAPTER 3

The Amazing Daughters of Shallum

Scripture: Nehemiah 1–4

Song: "God's Family"

Today's lesson is a wowser! When I really "saw" this story, my heart was so full. Why? My eyes beheld a story of women who were doing the work of men—and that was unusual. I love God, and the way He works! It thrills me that He loves me, a woman, just like He loves a man. A male chauvinist, God is not. He used men and women thousands of years ago to accomplish His purposes, and He does the very same thing today.

Rebuilding the wall surrounding Jerusalem was a huge and daunting task, not to mention the constant barrage of danger and "talking smack" coming from the other side. Demeaning it could have been, but God's people refused to let anything being hurled from Sanballat the Horonite or Tobiah the Ammonite stop them. Nehemiah 4:6 holds the key to the spirit of the Jews during this time period after the Babylonian captivity: "The people had a mind to work." God even tells us in Nehemiah 4:17 that all the workers had a weapon in one hand while building the wall with the other hand. How amazing is that!

How interesting it is to imagine the type and number of weapons these daughters could easily have hidden: one or two knives strapped to a thigh or tucked into a waistband or even a dagger in a shoe. Shallum, like any other father, would certainly have made sure his daughters had protection. Don't we wonder what other weapons these daughters could have used?

How interesting it is also to imagine what those fifty-two days of building the wall would have looked like. The "busyness" of an ant colony or a beehive quickly comes to mind. Can't you picture them? Hundreds of God's children scurrying to and fro with roughly made wheelbarrows full of stone and mortar; men and women shouting out commands and encouragement, with their eyes constantly darting along the walls and watching—eyes full of energy, determination, and faith. Surely this monumental effort to rebuild the wall of Jerusalem was truly an epic moment for the Jews, not seen since the crossing of the Red Sea!

> But God led Nehemiah to work on the walls, no less than he led Ezra to work on the temple. Both the sacred and the secular were necessary to fulfill God's plan to restore the nation of Israel. If the walls were unfinished, the temple was unfinished too. The work was of a single piece. The reason for this is easy to understand. Without a wall, no city in the ancient Near East was safe from bandits, gangs, and wild animals, even though the empire might be at peace. The more economically and culturally developed a city was, the greater the value of things in the city, and the greater the need for the wall. The temple, with its rich decorations, would have been particularly at risk. Practically speaking, no wall means no city, and no city means no temple.[1]

We may not know the names of these women, but God has made sure that we meet them and know the mighty task they accomplished for Him. Personally, I am just tickled to death that we encounter these girls of the Shallum clan (Neh. 3:12). They surely were their dad's right hands!

---

1 "Rebuilding the Wall of Jerusalem (Nehemiah 1:1–7:73)," Bible Commentary produced by Theology of Work Project. Accessed Jan. 12, 2024. https://www.theologofwork.org/old-testament/ezra-nehemiah-esther/nehemiah/restoration-of-the-wall-of-jerusalem-nehemiah-11-773/

TIME FOR A CLOSER LOOK

1. Give an approximate date for this event in Nehemiah.

2. Where and what is the main city?

3. What news did Nehemiah hear that made his heart so sad that he wept (Neh. 1:1–4)?

4. What was Nehemiah's job, and who was the king that he served (Neh. 1:11; 2:1)?

5. In what condition did Nehemiah find Jerusalem when he arrived from Susa? What did he decide to do (Neh. 2:17)?

6. What is the significance of the words "next to" in chapter 3? What do they describe?

_____

_____

_____

7. Copy Nehemiah 3:12. Why is this verse so outstanding?

_____

_____

_____

_____

8. What was Shallum's office? How many sons did he have?

_____

_____

_____

9. How did the Jews feel about building the wall (Neh. 4:6)?

_____

_____

_____

10. How did the outsiders feel about Nehemiah's building of the wall (Neh. 4:7–8)?

_____

_____

_____

11. What did the Jews do *first* when they found out the opposition's plan (Neh. 4:9)?

_____

_____

_____

12. What did Nehemiah do (Neh. 4:13, 17)?

13. Do you think Shallum and his daughters were armed as they worked? Why?

14. What kind of weapons would these girls have been able to handle?

15. Describe the task itself and describe the spirit among the workers. What did Nehemiah tell the workers in Nehemiah 4:20?

16. How many people were involved in building this wall, and who paid the expenses for it?

17. Read Nehemiah 4:7–23. Who were the enemies trying to stop the wall?

WHAT OTHERS HAVE SAID

Burton Coffman: The skill and ability of Nehemiah appear dramatically in this chapter. Even the High Priest, of all people, was enlisted in the work. Nobody was exempt; the entire population of Judah, some twenty-five or thirty thousand men, all went to work at one time on the city wall. No wonder it was finished in record time. . . .

Everybody engaged in the work. "All classes participated in the project, including priests (Neh. 3:1), goldsmiths and perfumers (Neh. 3:8), rulers of the city and even women (Neh. 3:12), also Levites (Neh. 3:17) and merchants (Neh. 3:32)" (*The New Bible Commentary*, Revised, p. 405).

Not merely the population of Jerusalem engaged in this project, but their fellow-countrymen who lived throughout the area. "These included the men of Jericho (Neh. 3:2), the Tekoites (v. 5), the men of Gibeon and Mizpah (v. 7), the inhabitants of Zanoah (v. 13), those who lived in the district of Bethzur (v. 16), those in Keilah (v. 17), and the men of the Plain, the Jordan valley (v. 22)" (*The New Layman's Bible Commentary*, p. 536).[2]

BOTTOM LINE

Why do you think God has given us this account of Shallum's daughters?

---

2 Burton Coffman, *Coffman's Commentaries on the Bible*, Nehemiah 3:1–3, accessed Jan. 11, 2024. https://www.studylight.org/commentaries/eng/bcc/nehemiah-3.html.

PRAYER

Dear Father, thank You from the bottom of our hearts for loving us and for blessing us every day. Thank You for our jobs, for our families, and for all those we love. We thank You especially for these unnamed daughters, our examples, from the book of Nehemiah who helped to accomplish such a great task as building a wall. Father, help us to accomplish great things for You and to look for opportunities to tell others about You and Your love. We are so grateful for Nehemiah's words: "Our God will fight for us." Most of all, we thank You for You and Your Word. We love being Your daughters. In Jesus' name, Amen.

WADING IN THE WATER

WOMEN WITH NO VOICE BUT THEIR OWN

I have always loved God's concept of the "family." Dad, Mom, brother, sister, parent, grandparent, uncle, aunt, niece, nephew, and cousin. Relatives. It's all good. And I have always loved the concept of family get-togethers—eating, gatherings, picnics, reunions. And that is good too.

However, as you and I well know, time flies and soon loved ones slip away from us. Children grow up, parents die, and things change. This is not always good.

My parents died seven months apart, and for me, that was heart rending. It seems I was standing by the casket of my father and then I turned, and again I was standing by the casket of my mother. A dear friend sent me a sympathy card expressing the sentiment I had heard all my life—that of being an orphan. She said, "Becky, you are nobody's child now."

I know what she was trying to say. I no longer had someone on this earth whom I could physically point out as being my mom or my dad. I was all alone. For a while I experienced certain unusual feelings: My rock was gone; I was unstable, and I was drowning. This is called grief . . . or at least it was my grief for a time.

To be honest, I never lost my faith in God. My love for Him never changed. But I was overwhelmed by all the emotions flooding my mind and soul. I felt so lonely. I no longer had the security of wise words freely given and constant affection. I missed Mom and Dad's voices. I missed their phone calls. I grieved a long time—does one ever fully recover?—but gradually, bit by bit, I started to come alive again.

You see, God knows all things, so He knows all about grief. He is omniscient, omnipresent, and omnipotent. My parents may have forsaken me by their deaths, but I knew that God would never forsake me. I could feel His marvelous presence beside me as I walked this new path, and I could feel His strength guiding me as He always had. He was still there, and He was the one who mattered the most.

When I think of the brave daughters of Zelophehad, I think of five precious girls who had lost everything. Their parents do not seem to be in the picture. At least we know their father was not. They all came to the tent of meeting—the church building, as we know it. And they wanted Moses to plead their case before God. Hearing all this were the priest, all the leaders, and the congregation. Again, where did this happen? At the doorway of the tent of meeting. Why there? Because that is where Moses held court and asked God for answers to the problems the Jews had after departing Egypt. Was God listening to Moses? Oh, yes.

We believe in the power of prayer. In the worst of times and in the best of times we fall to our knees and beg God for deliverance, for help, for peace and comfort. In this next lesson we meet five women, daughters of God, who boldly pleaded their case before Moses, the leader of the Israelites. They were courageous. They were fearless and gut honest. They were on their own, women with no voice but their own. And our God heard. Oh, the mighty lesson our Father teaches in this story! Here they are: Mahlah, Noah, Hoglah, Milcah, and Tirzah, the courageous daughters of Zelophehad.

CHAPTER

The Courageous And Bold Daughters Of Zelophehad

Scripture: Numbers 26:33; 27:1–11

Song: "Guide Me, O Thou Great Jehovah"

Several times in the Bible we see occasions where a woman cries out to God, and He compassionately listens and then grants her request. Only this time, there are five daughters who stand and plead their case before God and the children of Israel.

What do you do when you are a woman, and there is no one to help you? What do you do when your parents are gone and you feel such helplessness? You talk to God. And that is exactly what these five girls did. They had come out of Egypt with their father, but their father had died in the wilderness. There was no money in the inheritance package for them, as the Mosaic law stated that all of any inheritance went to the sons in the family. But the Zelophehad family had no sons, only daughters. What were these girls to do? Hunger was knocking on their door!

They went to the source—Moses at the tent of meeting. They couldn't talk to God one on one, but they could do the next best thing: They could give Moses their case and let him confer with Jehovah God. They had to go straight to the top, and Moses was their lawyer to state their case to God. We even are told in Numbers 27 that the entire congregation witnessed their request.

Read Numbers 27:5–7: "So Moses brought their case before the Lord. Then the Lord spoke to Moses, saying, 'The daughters of Zelophehad are right.'" Read that again: "The daughters of Zelophehad are right." Do you see any anger on God's part at their request? I see only kindness and mercy.

It takes a lot of courage to state your problems publicly and before an entire congregation. But that is exactly what these daughters did. They firmly stood and did what Joe Friday from *Dragnet* always was known to say: "Just the facts, ma'am." And our God heard.

TIME FOR A CLOSER LOOK

1. Give an approximate date of this occurrence.

   _____

2. Where did this event take place?

   _____

3. Name the daughters of Zelophehad and name their tribe.

   _____

   _____

   _____

   _____

   _____

4. To whom did these daughters present their case? Who heard their plea?

   _____

   _____

   _____

5. Why was Moses involved in this? When did this custom begin? (See Exodus 33:7–11.)

6. What was the tent of meeting?

7. Had Zelophehad been involved with the rebellion of Korah?

8. Tell the story of Korah (Numbers 16:1–35).

9. What is the first thing Moses did after hearing the daughters' plea?

10. How did God react, and what was His ruling for the daughters?

_____

_____

_____

11. What was the new ruling for the people of Israel from this point onward?

_____

_____

_____

12. How did these five girls show courage?

_____

_____

_____

_____

_____

_____

_____

WHAT OTHERS HAVE SAID

Burton Coffman: The law of the inheritance of daughters, in cases where they had no brother, was that the land should pertain to their father's brothers in perpetuity; and in case he had no brothers, it went to his uncles; and if there were no uncles, the "next of kin" inherited. The purpose of all this was to keep the land of Canaan within the tribes to whom it was originally allocated; that this was the case appears in Numbers 36 where the law was amended to prevent any marriage of the inheriting daughters outside of their tribe. The civilization of the ancient Jews was built upon the land; and it was a great crime for a Jew to part with his inheritance. The incident of Ahab and the vineyard of Naboth highlights this and also shows how mercilessly the evil kings of Israel destroyed the whole concept of inalienable ownership of the land.[1]

Herbert Lockyer: Banded together these daughters fought for and declared their rights to their deceased father's property and won a decision upheld by legal courts in law to this day. Their right of inheritance was decided in their favor because there was not male joint-heirs, and on the condition that they marry men within their own tribe.[2]

BOTTOM LNE

Why do you think we have this account in the Bible? Is it necessary?

_____

_____

_____

PRAYER

Our Father, over and over we want You to know how much we love and adore You. Please forgive our immature ways and childish minds. Help us to see You and Your magnificence in caring for us, delivering us, and changing our lives. We thank You for this story of Your mercy in hearing the cries of five desperate daughters. We thank You, thank You, thank You for hearing their prayers and our prayers. What would we do without You? We don't ever, ever want to know. In Jesus' name, Amen.

---

1 Burton Coffman, _Coffman's Commentaries on the Bible,_ Numbers 27:6, accessed Jan. 11, 2024. https://www.studylight.org/commentaries/eng/bcc/numbers-27.html.

2 Lockyer, Herbert, _All the Women of the Bible_ (Grand Rapids: Zondervan, 1988), p. 69.

WADING IN THE WATER

"THE LITTLEST MISSIONARY"

To be a slave is unimaginable for most of us these days. We live in a free society where we are not owned by anyone. Slavery is outlawed and freedoms loudly touted. We come and go as we wish and openly pursue various goals. If our pursuits are legal, no one stops us.

Most of us enter this world as crying infants lovingly cared for by families. A low percentage of babies and children are abandoned and neglected. The closest we come to slavery is by reading history books of civilizations, including our own country and the Bible. For thousands of years people all over the world owned other people. People sold their own children, and slavery was alive and well.

For Christians, the exposure to servants and masters occurs throughout our Bible education. Discussions in Bible classes broaden our knowledge about Roman culture with slaves who sometimes suffered greatly at the hands of their masters. Old Testament history reveals that slavery was often an honorable solution to certain circumstances, such as indebtedness.

Have you ever visited Charleston, South Carolina? In the center of this 350-year-old city is the slave market where men and women were sold on a daily basis. It is a sad place. A preacher recently described the word *redeemed* as actually depicting a slave market and imagining ourselves on that block of humiliating public display. Then Jesus steps up and sets us free. This description helped many of us understand true redemption. Freedom from slavery and freedom from sin are obvious spiritual parallels.

That is why the story of a little slave girl in 2 Kings is such a treasure. Most of us know the account of Naaman the leper from the Old Testament. It is a favorite of many Bible students, filled with details, action, deceit, retribution, and two amazing miracles. In Luke 4:27, Jesus even used this event to teach in His hometown, Nazareth. And every time we read Naaman's story, we meet her, the little Israelite girl whom God used to teach all of us life-changing lessons.

For some odd reason, this young girl was kind and loving to her master and mistress. Probably they were kind and loving to her. Did she have to mention that there was a cure for her sick master? No. Could she not have just kept quiet and never said a word? Certainly. But she didn't. She had a kind heart. Surrounded by foreign people and unfamiliar tasks and customs, this little girl showed the kindness of God. She was a true missionary.

You and I must never forget that when we obey the gospel of Jesus, we become slaves too. Jesus is our Master, and we are His servants forever. We have been redeemed, bought by the blood of the Lamb, and set free from the slavery of sin. However, we no longer are our own. Christ calls us to deny ourselves and pick up our crosses daily and follow Him. What kind of servant are you? What kind of slave am I? Are we faithful to our Master? Do we even know who He is? Are we like this Israelite slave who evidently talked about God wherever she went?

Little girl of Israel, I don't know your name, but I sure want to meet you someday. God certainly put you in that home in Syria for a reason. Perhaps Naaman and his wife were childless. Perhaps you were the only child in their home. God doesn't tell us. But this I do know: You changed your master's life forever and gave him hope. Your presence in the Scriptures has taught me many lessons. You are the epitome of a true and real servant of the Lord.

CHAPTER 5

Slave Girl With A Heart of Gold

Scripture: 2 Kings 5:1–27

Song: "On Bended Knee"

More than two thousand years ago, Jesus shocked the world when He announced, "But I say to you, love your enemies and pray for those who persecute you" (Matt. 5:44). This was a rousing statement, to be sure, and one that was the opposite of how mankind normally views things. It shocked the world then, and it still shocks us today. You see, it's a "dog eat dog" kind of world, and who in his or her right mind would ever go so far as to pray for an enemy—much less love one?

In the Old Testament we see this very thing in the shape and form of a brave little girl whose love changed, healed, and taught the "worldly world" about the true God.

Syria, also known as Aram, is our setting for this astonishing account. We have the name of the sick general in this story and the mighty prophet Elisha. But God doesn't tell us the name of the courageous slave girl who helped her master. There also are three servants in this healing story. As you are reading, note them and the significant part each one plays.

Naaman is a strong figure here, digging in his heels when it came to immersing himself in the muddy Jordan. The keys necessary to Naaman being healed were two: surrender and immersion. And these same keys are necessary for us to become Christians today. The Holy Spirit inspired Peter to write:

> Corresponding to that [Noah's family being brought safely through water], baptism now saves you—not the removal of dirt from the flesh, but an appeal to God for a good conscience—through the resurrection of Jesus Christ (1 Pet. 3:21).

Let each of us ask, "Am I like Naaman? Do I balk when God tells me what to do?" What will it take for you and me to learn humility like Naaman had to learn?

Let us open God's powerful Word and read about a wonderful illustration of a mighty foreign general who found the God of Israel. There is so much to be learned here in 2 Kings 5:1–27. And while we are reading about leprous Naaman, let's remember that even Jesus brings him into the New Testament in Luke 4.

TIME FOR A CLOSER LOOK

1. What is the approximate date here?

   _____

2. What locations were involved in this account? Discuss distances.

   _____

   _____

   _____

   _____

   _____

   _____

3. Who was the commander of the Syrian army?

   _____

   _____

   _____

4. Describe how this little girl had arrived at Naaman's house.

_____

_____

_____

5. What are some problems a teenage slave girl might encounter?

_____

_____

_____

6. Describe Naaman's influence. Also describe his problem.

_____

_____

_____

7. Who had blessed Naaman's success as a soldier and given him the Syrian victory? Why do you think He had done this?

_____

_____

_____

8. We do not know the age of this servant girl, but she knew someone who could help Naaman. Whom did she recommend? What did she report? To whom did she tell it? (Read 2 Kings 5:2–3.)

_____

_____

_____

9. Tell of Naaman's encounter with Elisha and his immersion in the Jordan.

_____

_____

_____

10. What happened when Naaman came up out of the water the seventh time? How long did it take for those results to occur?

_____

_____

_____

11. What happens when we come up out of the water of baptism? (See Acts 2:38; 22:16.)

_____

_____

_____

12. If we want to be healed, forgiven, and saved, we must _____ God, just as Naaman did.

13. Imagine what Naaman's homecoming was like. What do you see in your mind?

_____

_____

_____

14. Find the three slaves in this story. Only one name is revealed. Describe them—their similarities and their differences.

_____

_____

_____

_____

WHAT OTHERS HAVE SAID

Burton Coffman: The unsung heroine of this whole narrative is this precious little girl who had been captured by the Syrians and made a slave to the house of Naaman. Instead of becoming bitter against her exploiters and harboring an undying hatred of them, she accepted her fate with meekness and exhibited deep friendship and sympathy with her mistress and her husband Naaman.

It was this captive maiden who enlightened the great lord of the Syrian armies of the existence of a true prophet of God in Samaria and of his ability to cure leprosy.

What an exhortation is this for everyone to seize all opportunities to speak of God and His great power to benefit sinful and suffering humanity! Through the word of this servant girl, the king of Syria received the knowledge of a true prophet of God in Samaria, information which was not even known (because of his own fault) by the king of Israel (Joram). . . .

It was no easy thing that Naaman did here. His dipping seven times in Jordan had been accomplished on his way back to Syria, at least some twenty miles from Samaria, and some scholars say thirty miles. Making the whole round trip with the animal-drawn conveyances of that era was a matter of several days additional travel. It is therefore a mark of Naaman's character and of his high appreciation for the miracle God had performed on his behalf that he would undertake this additional travel to return to Samaria.[1]

Adam Clarke: A little maid—who, it appears, had pious parents, who brought her up in the knowledge of the true God. Behold the goodness and the *severity* of the divine providence! Affectionate parents are deprived of their promising daughter by a set of lawless freebooters, without the smallest prospect that she should have any lot in life but that of misery, infamy, and woe.

Waited on Naaman's wife.—Her decent orderly behaviour, the consequence of her sober and pious education, entitled her to this place of distinction; in which her servitude was at least easy, and her person safe.

If God permitted the parents to be deprived of their pious child by the hands of ruffians, he did not permit the child to be without a

---

1 Burton Coffman, *Coffman's Commentaries on the Bible,* 2 Kings 5:1, 15, accessed Jan. 12, 2024. https://www.studylight.org/commentaries/eng/bcc/2-kings-5.html.

guardian. In such a case, were even the father and mother to forsake her, God would take her up. . . . By the captivity of this little maid, one Syrian family at least, and that one of the most considerable in the Syrian empire, is brought to the knowledge of the true God.[2]

BOTTOM LINE

Why does God give us the story of Naaman the leper and include the information concerning the little slave girl? What would you have done if you had been the slave girl?

_____

_____

_____

_____

PRAYER

Oh our Father, please forgive us of our sinful ways and thoughts. Help us to see Your marvelous love and the blessings You pour down upon our heads daily. Lord, may we always see the glory of knowing and obeying the gospel of Jesus. Thank You for giving us the opportunity of hearing and obeying it. Please be merciful with us and please let us be courageous in telling others the Good News. Help us to see others the way You do and to be humble. Please, please help us to "walk by faith and not by sight." We love You with all our hearts. In Jesus' name, Amen.

2 Adam Clarke, *Clarke's Commentary,* 2 Kings 5:2–3, accessed Jan. 12, 2024. https://www .studylight.org/commentaries/eng/acc/2-kings-5.html.

WADING IN THE WATER

GOD HAS A PLAN

My dear friend Helen had asked me to tend to her plants while she was out of town for several days. No problem. I can water plants, but being a gardener who knows her way around plants, joyously digging in the dirt, I am not. I drove over to Helen's house on a very hot summer morning, and from then on, that was the only quiet thing that would occur for the next several hours—just driving. Arriving at sweet Helen's house, the nightmare began.

On arrival, I got the key from under the rocker on the porch, unlocked the door, and went into the house. I put my purse and key down, and then, cell phone in hand, went out the patio door and closed it. I found all the hoses and watered the living daylights out of those plants. I was a good girl. Got through and put up the hoses. Done. Did I mention it was a hot summer day?

I turned to leave through the patio door. Locked. Locked? What? My purse is inside and the car keys! Front door is locked; patio door is locked; garage door is locked. When I called Helen, she did tell me this: "Becky, that happens to us occasionally. That side door just locks itself."

Did I tell you that it was very hot and getting hotter? I called the locksmith, then sat down on the backyard swing to cool off. Slowly I rocked and waited while a soft breeze continued to blow. I was God's captive; I found myself talking to Him, praying for others, and thanking Him, especially for this moment when I could just stop and look at Him through His creation. Flowers, green grass, birds, children nearby laughing—these are the sights and sounds of God, my friends.

Finally, the locksmith appeared, and of course, trying to open the locked patio door became an ordeal for him. Nothing was going to be easy this day. What else could go wrong? He used all kinds of devices, but nothing was working. The lock just would not cooperate. He and I talked about God.

"I am praying for you," I said.

"I am Mormon—but not a good one," he stated.

I invited him to church. He offered, "I don't like the King James Version of the Bible."

"That's okay, there are other versions, but the King James Version Bible will tell anybody how to get to heaven."

I kept begging God inside my head to give me the right words—something to help this man and his feelings about God's Word. I went around the corner of the garage, out of sight, and got on my knees and prayed softly as he worked so diligently. I prayed for him to find God, his place in this life, for the Lord to use me, and of course, that locked patio door.

This task of unlocking the door took more time than usual. I wondered about that. Could it be, as I reflected later, that the Lord wanted me to meet this particular locksmith that day? Was that His plan? My plan was to water the plants and scoot home. But God had something else in mind. It was to meet a stranger who intersected my path, who needed to know about God's message and where that message could be studied. And that is where ol' Beck came in. All I did was point the way; what that stranger did with it was up to him.

My friend, our mighty God has a vineyard where His willing servants do His bidding. Christians are a part of God's work. He uses us to share the light, share the gospel, and share the love of Jesus. God lays opportunity after opportunity constantly at our feet to save a lost and dying world. We must be on our toes. God is watching us. God is testing us. God is using us. The Holy Spirit speaks through Paul and reminds us, "I planted, Apollos watered, but God gave the increase" (1 Cor. 3:6 NKJV).

So get ready for a curve ball of opportunity. It may come out of left field on a hot, frustrating, summer day, but trust me, it will come. And often. That is just how God works. So we should say, "Thank You, my Father—what an indescribable honor it is to be used by You!"

Now let us meet a woman who was part of God's plan to accomplish a better life for Israel, His cherished child. She used her opportunity in a most unique way.

CHAPTER

Don't Mess with Jael: A Woman's Mighty Arm

Scripture: Judges 1:16; 4:1–22; 5:24–27

Song: "Praise the Lord"

I am always amazed at this story of Jael, wife of Heber, the Kenite, who so magnificently, swiftly, and violently destroyed a ruthless leader. It was a graphic event, true—but remember it was prophesied! With Deborah and the judges of Israel in the background, we find a woman put in a peculiar set of circumstances.

This particular account of the battle between the Israelites and the Canaanites at the Kishon River requires quite a bit of digging and asking a lot of questions. Jael's life was bound to her husband's heritage and choices. They were Kenites.

Let's consider some facts:

🌱 Heber, the Kenite, is a prominent background figure in this story. Judges 1:16 tells us that the Kenites were descendants of Moses' father-in-law and dwelt among the tribe of Judah.

🌱 Judges 4:11 gives us the added information that Heber had separated himself from the Kenites and had pitched his tent near Kedesh. Some scholars think that Heber and Jael had relocated because of a recent Philistine invasion.

🌿 There was peace between Heber and Jabin, the king of Hazor (Judg. 4:17). What does that mean? Heber and Jabin knew one another and lived peaceably in the same area.

🌿 One meaning of Heber's name is "ally," and "Kenite" identified him as belonging to a clan of metalworkers. It is possible that Heber moved north to ally himself with Jabin, the Canaanite king who had iron chariots (Judg. 4:13).

Using a Bible encyclopedia and dictionary, find the fact that the Kenites were metalworkers. Also, note any other facts of interest.

_____

_____

_____

It certainly makes sense that Heber would move away from the Israelites in order to do business with the enemy, Jabin the king, specifically regarding iron chariots. Probably, Heber would not have had the support of his kinsmen, the Israelites, in his fraternizing with the enemy. Remember, Heber was not descended from any of the tribes of Israel, but his ancestors were from Midian, and the father of the Midianites was Abraham.

THE ISRAELITE'S TRIUMPH

Picture the battle scene. Remember, Deborah, the only woman judge of Israel, has bravely gone into this battle with the fearful Barak. God often has a surprise up His sleeve, so watch what He does here. While Barak is leading ten thousand Israelites *down* Mt. Tabor, Sisera is leading nine hundred chariots and men *toward* Mt. Tabor. God brings these two mighty armies together in a furious clash at the Kishon River south of the mountain.

How did Israel win the battle? (Read Judges 4:15.)

_____

_____

_____

How did God accomplish this? (Read Judges 5:20–21.)

_____

_____

_____

Consider the following observation and note why you agree or disagree.

> Heber's wife, Jael, called Sisera into her tent with the promise of safety (Judg. 4:18). Sisera accepted her offer. Since it was against social norms for a man to enter a woman's tent, Jael seemed to be offering a perfect hiding place.[1]

_____

_____

_____

Our mighty God was not finished. It was a day of "ones." One woman judge, one battle, one river, one powerful storm, one man running for his life, and lastly, one clever woman with one hammer and one tent peg.

Do you know the account of Jael and her powerful right hand? Get into the Word and dig deeply to discover a woman God used to achieve a victory for Israel. Believe me, this is the woman you want on your side! Trust me, you will not forget her.

TIME FOR A CLOSER LOOK

1. When did this event take place?

_____

_____

_____

1 "Who Was Sisera in the Bible?" *Got Questions Ministries*, Jan. 4, 2022. https://www.gotquestions.org/Sisera-in-the-Bible.html.

2. Where is the location of the battle?

3. What was the relationship between Israel and God? What was the prophecy Deborah had told Barak about the one who would kill Sisera?

4. How did God rout Sisera and the Canaanites? (See Judges 5:21.)

5. What did Sisera do and why would he head toward the tent of Heber and Jael? Why would it provide safety for him? (See Judges 4:17.)

6. What kind of manner did Jael have when she went out to meet Sisera? What did she convince him to do?

7. What kindnesses did Jael show to Sisera in Judges 4:18–19?

8. Why didn't Sisera stay awake and see what Jael was attempting to do? The New American Standard Bible 1995 says she "secretly" went to Sisera (Judg. 4:21). What does that mean?

_____

_____

_____

_____

9. Who else did Jael invite into her tent that day and why?

_____

_____

_____

10. What adjectives would you use to describe Jael?

_____

_____

_____

11. Jael evidently invites both of the leaders in this story to her tent, but whose side does she favor?

_____

_____

_____

12. Why should Jael feel compelled to kill Sisera? (Judges 4:7, 9, 14, and 15.)

_____

_____

_____

WHAT OTHERS HAVE SAID

Burton Coffman: It is said that the business of pitching and striking the tent was usually assigned to the women among the nomads, and Jael, therefore, would have been quite skilled in the use of this equipment. . . .

Speaking of the morality of this action on Jael's part, what can be said? The falsehood, treachery, deception, and cold-blooded murder appearing in this event can only be denounced as sinful, and yet there were surely mitigating circumstances. We can admire Jael's courage, her love of the people of God, and her audacious action in taking the life of their chief enemy. It is nowhere indicated in the Bible that God approved of Jael's behavior in this episode. The prophecy that something like this would surely happen cannot be interpreted as God's approval of how it happened. Still, in the next chapter, Deborah referred to Jael as "blessed"; and Jael herself appeared to be quite happy with her achievement as she showed Sisera's body to Barak.[2]

Adam Clarke: He preferred the woman's tent because of secrecy; for, according to the etiquette of the eastern countries, no person ever intrudes into the apartments of the women. And in every dwelling the women have a separate apartment.[3]

BOTTOM LINE

We always cheer when the bad guy is killed in the movies. What about here? One more time, read Judges 4:9, 14 and 1 Samuel 12:6–9 and

2 Burton Coffman, *Coffman's Commentaries on the Bible*, Judges 4:21, accessed Jan. 12, 2024. https://www.studylight.org/commentaries/eng/bcc/judges-4.html.

3 Adam Clarke, *Clarke's Commentary*, Judges 4:18, accessed Jan. 12, 2024. https://www.studylight.org/commentaries/eng/acc/judges-4.html.

find the key to this account. Any thoughts on why God has given us her story?

_____

_____

_____

PRAYER

Our most precious Father, thank You for the many times in our lives when You have delivered us from danger, bad relationships, and troubling times. Thank You for understanding all the things about us—even when we don't understand what is happening in our lives and what we should do. We trust in You, our Father. Please use us to accomplish Your purposes in this life—just as You did with Jael. We know how much You love and care for us, Your sheep. Help us to walk with You and only You. Please don't stop loving us, and please don't stop guiding us. In Jesus' name, Amen.

WADING IN THE WATER

"WEEPING OVER GROWN CHILDREN"

When I read the story of Rizpah, our next woman of surprise, I actually have no words. The first time I met her, I read, reread, and reread her account. I tried to dig and asked questions that were pertinent to the story. Why were the Gibeonites so angry, and why had Saul been so bloodthirsty? I put myself in her place and envisioned the day when David's soldiers walked into her home, grabbed her two sons, and left for their execution. What could she do to stop them? Absolutely nothing. I cannot imagine the desperateness she must have felt as she possibly saw them killed and exposed for all to see. How do you process that? How was anything ever normal again?

In my mind, I see her urgently and devotedly screaming and flinging her arms and body over and over to scare the animals and birds away from her sons' bodies. Months and months go by. Surely Rizpah resembles a harpy, the terrifying bird-woman of Greek mythology. In my mind she is the picture of pure exhaustion, unkempt hair and clothes—a crazed look in her eyes. She is intent on her mission, every night and every day, doing what always came naturally—taking care of her children. She was a mother, and these were her sons. Alive or dead, they were still hers, and she could not let go.

In life she was unable to stop their deaths. She was a woman. The king was the ruler; she was not. But this one thing she could do: she could watch over her boys, day by day and hour by hour, until there was nothing left of them but bones. And even then, she would never leave them. They were still "bone of her bones and flesh of her flesh." That sackcloth covered rock was going to be her home until she drew her last breath.

What is it like to see your child die? May I never know, and may you never know either. I cannot help but think of Mary, standing at the cross with John and the other women who loved Jesus almost as much as she did. How her heart must have broken as she saw Him suffer, bleed, and die. He was the Savior of the world, and yet He was the child she carried and loved before He ever set foot on this earth. He was the baby in the manger, the boy in the temple, the miracle worker who turned the world upside down.

There is one thing I always think of as I read about you, Rizpah, my sister. I would do the very same thing for my son or my daughter. My heart weeps for you. We are alike in that we feel that our children belong in our arms forever. And that is all that ever matters.

Rizpah's story is one of a kind. It's one of the saddest in God's precious Word. There is a reason God lets us see her, so let's open our Bible and discover this very special mother in Israel.

CHAPTER 7

Rizpah: One Tragic Heartbroken Mother!

Scripture: 2 Samuel 21:1–14

Song: "It Is Well with My Soul"

Not all stories in the Bible have a happy beginning and ending. Not all stories are "feel good" stories—tales of justice and fairness. Sometimes stories are shocking, violent, and at the same time heart-rending. So is this account of a woman and her two dead sons.

Do you remember the Gibeonites and how they had deceived Israel? Many years had passed since the deception, but Saul had violently taken revenge on them to please Israel and Judah. Like He had done in the past, God sent a famine upon Israel as punishment. Without consulting God, David goes to the Gibeonites and asks them for a resolution to the problem, agrees with it, and then performs it. Enter Rizpah.

God lets us see what lengths Rizpah goes to in order to keep her sons' bodies protected—not one or two days or weeks, but months. Who can imagine what this woman does?

This account not only is hard to read, but it also is full of raw emotion—even for the hardest of hearts. God wants us to know her story. Let's stop, meet, and think about Rizpah.

TIME FOR A CLOSER LOOK

1. Approximately what year is it?

2. What are the locations in this story?

3. According to 2 Samuel 21:1, why was there a famine in the land? Who prayed and asked God why?

4. What adjective does God use to describe the house of Saul in 2 Samuel 21:1?

5. What had the Gibeonites done to Israel in Joshua 9:3–27? Read the account together.

6. Who personally goes and speaks to the Gibeonites (2 Sam. 21:2)? Was this the right thing to do?

_____

_____

_____

7. Regarding the Gibeonites, Joshua and his men did not ask for the counsel of _____ (Josh. 9:14). What can we learn from this example?

_____

_____

_____

8. Discuss the kind of death these men received (2 Sam. 21:6).

_____

_____

_____

9. Name the two sons of Rizpah who were slain. From where were the others taken? Who was Rizpah, and how do we know this was not from Michal, David's first wife? (See 2 Samuel 6:15–23.)

_____

_____

_____

10. What time of year did this event happen? How long did Rizpah keep her watch over her sons? What did she not allow to happen? What was the sackcloth for?

_____

_____

_____

11. Using the internet, research Rizpah and look at the artists' paintings of this event in the Bible. What is your feedback?

_____

_____

_____

_____

12. How did David find out about Rizpah's actions, and what did he do personally?

_____

_____

_____

13. Where were these sons most likely buried? What does it say about God in 2 Samuel 21:13–14?

_____

_____

_____

14. Rizpah never says a word in this most tragic account. How is her silence deafening?

_____

_____

_____

_____

WHAT OTHERS HAVE SAID

Burton Coffman: "The meaning of the word *hang* here is unknown" (Arthur S. Peake's Commentary, p. 292). It is generally believed to be some brutal, inhuman torturing death often practiced among heathen people. Furthermore, they left the bodies exposed from March 21 to the time of the autumn rains, directly contrary to and a wanton violation of God's Word (Deut. 21:22–23). . . .

Having been condemned by Israel to perpetual slavery, why did they not ask for an end of that? Instead, they wished to torture the sons of Saul! Not until the request of Salome, who turned down half a kingdom to choose instead the head of John the Baptist, is there anything in the Bible that matches this insane request of the Gibeonites. As Matthew Henry said, "They had a fair opportunity to get rid of their servitude, but they did not take it" (Matthew Henry's Commentary, Vol. 2, p. 556).

God indeed promised that the sins of one generation might indeed be the reason for punishment of succeeding generations, but there is no record where God ever extended this privilege of executing innocents for the crimes of their ancestors into the hands of mortal and fallible men. These men David turned over to the Gibeonites were not sons of Saul in the ordinary sense, but grandsons, and there never was a divine law that allowed men to execute grandsons for the crimes of their grandfather. . . .

"The rains usually came in late November or early December, so Rizpah must have kept a six-months vigil over the bodies" (John T. Willis, p. 400).[1]

Wil Gafney: Rizpah bat Aiah watches the corpses of her sons stiffen, soften, swell, and sink into the stench of decay . . . fights with winged, clawed, and toothed scavengers night and day. She is there from the spring harvest until the fall rains, as many as six months from Nissan

---

1 Burton Coffman, *Coffman's Commentaries on the Bible*, 2 Samuel 21:6, 10, accessed Jan. 12, 2024. https://www.studylight.org/commentaries/eng/bcc/2-samuel-21.html.

(March/April) to Tishrei (September/October), sleeping, eating, toileting, protecting, and bearing witness.[2]

Mother O' Mine

If I were hanged on the highest hill,
Mother o' mine, O mother o' mine!
I know whose love would follow me still,
Mother o' mine, O mother o' mine!

If I were drowned in the deepest sea,
Mother o' mine, O mother o' mine!
I know whose tears would come down to me,
Mother o' mine, O mother o' mine!

If I were damned of body and soul,
I know whose prayers would make me whole,
Mother o' mine, O mother o' mine!

—Rudyard Kipling

BOTTOM LINE

What would you have done if you had been Rizpah? Why does God tell us her story?

---

2 Wil Gafney, *Womanist Midrash: A Reintroduction to the Women of the Torah and the Throne* (Louisville: Westminster John Knox Press, 2017), 200–201.

PRAYER

Precious Father, thank You for loving us and healing our hearts when we are broken and grieving—especially over our children. Like David wrote about You, we repeat to ourselves over and over the words from Psalm 51:17: "The sacrifices of God are a broken spirit; a broken and a contrite heart, O God, You will not despise." O God, so many times in this life, we are so sad that we just want to give up. We understand Rizpah's broken heart. We look to You, our Father, for help. We turn to You, our Father, for comfort. Only You can restore our soul. We love, love, love You, Father. Please help us. Please heal our broken hearts. In Jesus' name, Amen.

WADING IN THE WATER

GOD'S GOT A HEDGE

I once worked for a terrific lady boss. She was sympathetic, understanding, and religious. There was a phrase that she would use frequently when describing her son. She would say, "The Lord has His hand on him!" I wasn't quite sure what she meant—until one day during my reading I discovered Psalm 139:5: "You have enclosed me behind and before, and laid Your hand upon me."

I found the phrase my friend repeatedly used!

Verse 5 is a description of the comfort hedge that David wrote about and what we Christians often discuss. There is a hedge—protection—around us, placed there by God Himself. This scripture says so—very simply. David again wrote about this hedge in Psalm 5:12, "For it is You who blesses the righteous man, O Lord, You surround him with favor as with a shield." Satan also remarked about the hedge around Job: "Have You not made a hedge about him and his house and all that he has, on every side?" (Job 1:10).

But wait, there is more. On top of that hedge, God has placed His marvelous hand, holding us in place. The commentary writer, Albert Barnes, once wrote this about David's 139th Psalm: "God was on every side of him; that he could not escape in any direction."[1]

Knowing that our Father loves us enough to surround us, to encompass us on all sides with His protection and then to cover us with His own hand is absolutely what David continued to say

---

1   Albert Barnes, *Barnes' Notes on the Whole Bible*, Psalm 139:5, accessed Jan. 12, 2024. https://www.studylight.org/commentaries/eng/bnb/psalms-139.html.

in Psalm 139:6: "Such knowledge is too wonderful for me; it is too high, I cannot attain [comprehend] to it." Yes, Lord, it is more than I can take in. Doesn't this wonderful psalm make us love God even more? And what comfort this song is to all who read it. As a mother, I pray for that incredible hedge to stay around me and my family. I know you do too.

I just thought you and I needed a reminder today of the indescribable power of the One who loves us the most and that marvelous shield called our *hedge*. Oh, and one more thing we needed to be reminded of today—to say, "Thank You, God."

Coming up is the story of two women who defied a king and were protected and rewarded by God for it. Now that's bold! Let's take courage from the assurance that God's hand is upon us and live boldly just as these women did!

CHAPTER 8

Shiphrah and Puah: Saviors of a Nation

Scriptures: Exodus 1:15–22

Song: "Faith Is the Victory"

Standing up to Yul Brynner the actor would be a real challenge, I think. If you are of a certain age, you grew up on *The Ten Commandments* starring Charlton Heston as Moses and Yul Brynner as Pharaoh. Both men were convincing in their portrayals respectively of Moses, the leader of the Israelites, and Pharaoh, the stubborn king of Egypt. But imagine you are a woman, refusing to obey Pharaoh's edict about murdering the Hebrew male babies and living to tell about it. The word *gutsy* comes to mind. But it is more than that.

Few of us know the names of these two Hebrew women who skillfully defied Pharaoh's commands of killing and drowning the newborn males of Israel. What a horrible time this was for the Israelites and their young families! But God had a plan for these Hebrew children to multiply, grow strong, and flee Egypt.

God also had a plan for Shiphrah and Puah. Boldy they obeyed God instead of the king of Egypt. Only God knows how many lives they saved and all because of their faith in Jehovah God. May we never forget, too, that God blessed them for standing up to Pharaoh. Oh, what lessons there are here for the Christian who wants to do the right thing!

Stop and ponder if you would have had their courage. Come and meet Shiphrah and Puah, two midwives who feared God and were just as stubborn as the king of the Nile.

TIME FOR A CLOSER LOOK

1. When did this event occur?

_____

_____

_____

2. What is the location?

_____

_____

_____

3. Who are Shiphrah and Puah, and what is their nationality?

_____

_____

_____

4. Write out Exodus 1:16.

_____

_____

_____

5. What is the literal term for birthstool?

_____

_____

_____

6. Why did these women not obey Pharaoh?

_____

_____

_____

7. What reasons did they give Pharaoh for not obeying his orders? Were these reasons completely true?

_____

_____

_____

_____

8. As a result, God was _____ to the midwives, and the people _____ (Exod. 1:20).

9. What did God do for these women (v. 21)? This verse reminds us that all this happened because the midwives feared God. How can you apply this to your life today?

_____

_____

_____

10. What are the similarities found in Matthew 2:13–16?

_____

_____

_____

11. Did Shiphrah and Puah do the right thing? Defend your answer.

_____

_____

_____

WHAT OTHERS HAVE SAID

Burton Coffman: Although the entire testimony of these midwives must be considered false, because the primary purpose of it was to deceive Pharaoh, it is also evident that essential elements of fact were included in their reply. It was true that the Hebrew women were unlike the Egyptian women, as attested by pictures excavated from the ancient tombs and dated about 1400 BC, showing that the Egyptian women were more delicate and essentially smaller in stature. The big-boned Hebrew female slaves are depicted wearing heavy garments and obviously possessing much more vigor than the Egyptians. It was false, of course, that the Hebrew women were delivered before the midwives could assist them.

It is amazing that some students find it hard to understand how God could have rewarded such liars! However, we find no difficulty with such a question. God rewarded those midwives, not for their falsehood to Pharaoh, but for their fear of God and for their aiding his purpose of multiplying the Israelites. In this first encounter between God and Pharaoh, God was gloriously victorious, just as would be the case in all subsequent phases of the conflict. . . .

The most astounding thing about this event is that the very action which Pharaoh took in his purpose of destroying Israel was exactly the thing that placed a Hebrew man-child in the very bosom of the king's family, making him, at last, the heir to Pharaoh's throne! How past finding out are the ways of God! Where in the literature of any nation, or of all nations, is there anything to approach the inspired drama of what leaps up before us in Exodus?[2]

2 Burton Coffman, *Coffman's Commentaries on the Bible*, Exodus 1:19–22, accessed Jan. 12, 2024. https://www.studylight.org/commentaries/eng/bcc/exodus-1.html.

BOTTOM L|NE

Why is this story so important? What would you have done?

_____

_____

_____

_____

PRAYER

Dear Father, thank You for this story of two women who feared You and refused to obey evil. Please help us to do the very same thing. Help us to be bold in our faith—unafraid to stand for what is right in Your sight. Help us to tell others of Your love, mercy, and grace. Give us the courage to love You more than anything else and just stay the course. May we always remember Your marvelous hedge around us is alive and well. We love You, precious Father. In Jesus' name, Amen.

WADING IN THE WATER

THE ROAD NOT TAKEN

It's hard not to love the poetry of Robert Frost. Having been raised in New England, I can picture the scenery, the animals, and the ways of New Englanders in every line. Perhaps many of you already have a favorite of his work. One of his most popular poems is the one below.

The Road Not Taken

Two roads diverged in a yellow wood,
And sorry I could not travel both
And be one traveler, long I stood
And looked down one as far as I could
To where it bent in the undergrowth;

Then took the other, as just as fair,
And having perhaps the better claim,
Because it was grassy and wanted wear;
Though as for that the passing there
Had worn them really about the same,

And both that morning equally lay
In leaves no step had trodden black.
Oh, I kept the first for another day!
Yet knowing how way leads on to way,
I doubted if I should ever come back.

I shall be telling this with a sigh
Somewhere ages and ages hence:
Two roads diverged in a wood, and I—
I took the one less traveled by,
And that has made all the difference.

—Robert Frost, 1915

Is there a human among us who has not at one time or another pondered upon the course of his or her life and wondered if things could have turned out differently? All the intriguing what-ifs can toy with one's brain, that is for sure. We all ask ourselves questions like: What if I hadn't gone to that summer camp? What if I had met so and so first? If I had it to do over again, would I want to be where I am now?

The Father in heaven has a plan for all of us.

> "For I know the plans that I have for you," declares the Lord, "plans for welfare and not for calamity to give you a future and a hope. Then you will call upon Me and come and pray to Me, and I will listen to you. You will seek Me and find Me when you search for Me with all your heart" (Jer. 29:11–13).

God was talking to His children in this passage, and I believe that the passage reaches across the ages in admonition to His children today.

Knowing the Lord has a plan for me reassures me of His love for me, present and future. I have learned in my old age not to fight God—just go where He directs and leads. After all, He has said it loudly and clearly in Psalm 32:8: "I will instruct you and teach you in the way which you should go; I will counsel you with My eye upon you."

The Father has never failed me. He is faithful. I must trust Him and let Him take care of the details.

Let's look at a woman who had the opportunity to travel a different road and did not take it. I always wonder if she regretted it all the days of her life.

CHAPTER 9

Orpah, Think Again!

Scriptures: Ruth 1:1–18
Song: "Each Step I Take"

L
ike all the characters in this particular Bible study, we do not know much about Orpah. God allows us to see her in approximately thirteen verses of the book of Ruth.

We cherish the romantic love story of Ruth—the Moabitess whom God blessed and placed in the lineage of Christ. But what do we know about Orpah, Ruth's sister-in-law, another Moabitess? Let's remember that she, like Ruth, had also lost her husband. Surely her heart was broken and empty. She loved Naomi, but in the end, she chose to go back to her family, her gods, and her old life. Orpah did not choose to live the rest of her life in Bethlehem. We do not hear from her ever again. We can only hope she found another good husband and had a family, but we simply do not know.

Ruth, on the other hand, was blessed with the mighty hand of God with a rich husband, a wonderful mother-in-law, a baby, a village, and best of all—she earned an honored spot in the bloodline of God's Son, Jesus. What an honor God bestowed upon her!

Crack open that Bible, friends, and let's dig and learn.

TIME FOR A CLOSER LOOK

1. When does this story occur?

   _____

   _____

   _____

2. Where are the locations in this story?

   _____

   _____

   _____

3. Naomi had traveled to _____ because of a _____ .
   Why does a move of necessity often cause great distress?

   _____

   _____

4. Where was Naomi from and whom had she married?

   _____

   _____

   _____

5. Let's do some digging and note the meanings of names here. Write down the meaning of Naomi, Elimelech, Mahlon, and Chilion. Are they descriptive? Find the meanings of Ruth and Orpah.

   _____

   _____

   _____

6. What does Bethlehem mean, and why is this ironic now?

   _____

   _____

   _____

7. How long did Naomi, Ruth, and Orpah live in this area of Moab? Describe the tragedies that befell them.

_____

_____

_____

_____

8. What does Naomi insist that the two daughters-in-law do?

_____

_____

_____

9. What decision does Ruth make?

_____

_____

_____

10. What decision does Orpah make?

_____

_____

_____

11. Who was the main god that Orpah and Ruth worshiped as children?

_____

_____

_____

12. What emotions do you see in this story of three women? How do you relate to them?

_____

_____

_____

13. What kind of relationship did Naomi have with her two daughters-in-law?

_____

_____

_____

WHAT OTHERS HAVE SAID

Burton Coffman: "Then she kissed them, and they lifted up their voices and wept" (Ruth 1:9). This indicates that the little company had reached the border, or the turning point, from which the friendly escort might have turned back. The simple meaning here is that Naomi kissed her daughters-in-law goodbye.

This paragraph introduces us to the author's characteristic device of using conversations to carry forward the thread of his narrative. Morris stated, "Over fifty out of the total of eighty-five verses in the whole book are taken up with dialogue" (Leon Morris, _Tyndale Old Testament Commentaries_, p. 253).

"They lifted up their voices and wept" (Ruth 1:9). This was the tearful prelude to the dialogue that followed. The moment of truth had come; it was time for the loving courteous escort of Naomi on the way to Judah to be terminated, but the human emotions over-flowed in a fountain of tears, the implication being that all three of them wept together.

"And they said, Nay, but we will return with thee unto thy people" (Ruth 1:10). Both daughters-in-law, at first, decided to go with Naomi to Judah, but Naomi wisely tried to dissuade them. As Moabitesses, they might not have received any welcome whatever in Israel![1]

---

1 Burton Coffman, _Coffman's Commentaries on the Bible_, Ruth 1:9–10, accessed Jan. 12, 2024. https://www.studylight.org/commentaries/eng/bcc/Ruth-1.html.

Matthew Henry: They were both so kind as to accompany her, some part of the way at least, when she returned towards the land of Judah. Her two daughters-in-law did not go about to persuade her to continue in the land of Moab, but, if she was resolved to go home, would pay her all possible civility and respect at parting; and this was one instance of it: they would *bring her on her way,* at least to the utmost limits of their country, and help her to carry her luggage as far as they went, for it does not appear that she had any servant to attend her (Ruth 1:7). By this we see both that Naomi, as became an Israelite, had been very kind and obliging to them and had won their love, in which she is an example to all mothers-in-law, and that Orpah and Ruth had a just sense of her kindness, for they were willing to return it thus far. It was a sign they had dwelt together in unity, though *those* were dead by whom the relation between them came. Though they retained an affection for the gods of Moab (Ruth 1:15), and Naomi was still faithful to the God of Israel, yet that was no hindrance to either side from love and kindness, and all the good offices that the relation required. Mothers-in-law and daughters-in-law are too often at variance (Matthew 10:35), and therefore it is the more commendable if they live in love; let all who sustain this relation aim at the praise of doing so.[2]

BOTTOM LINE

Why is this story so unusual? Would you have gone with Naomi?

---

2 Matthew Henry, *Henry's Complete Commentary on the Bible,* Ruth 1:7, 15, accessed Jan. 12, 2024. https://www.studylight.org/commentaries/eng/mhm/Ruth-1.html.

PRAYER

Our Father, thank You so much for this wonderful story of love, honor, and commitment. We shall always wonder what kind of life Orpah had when she left Naomi. We pray that it was a life filled with Your knowledge and Your presence. Help us to walk with You and talk with You with each step we take. Help us to always re-evaluate our life's current walk and align it with your steps. Please don't forget about us. We love You so much, and we live for You. In Jesus' name, Amen.

WADING IN THE WATER

I HAVE A QUESTION!

It's a daily battle, this life. Wake up; go to work; be nice; don't say what you think; be kind; be a blessing; make a difference; don't say it; change your attitude; help change someone else's attitude; watch yourself; watch your words; watch your behavior; be nice! And when the day is over, it is: Did I pass the test? Was I kind? Was I Jesus? I can do better tomorrow. God will help me.

The Christian is the most blessed person there ever will be in this world. She has heard and believed the gospel of Jesus; she has named the name of Jesus in confession; she has repented of her sins, and lastly, she has been buried with Jesus in baptism. If she is faithful, every day she lives after this is a God-given blessing because she is headed down heaven's road. Her life is not perfect because she is not perfect. Yes, she will have heartaches and troubles, but God is always there, walking by her side. What can man do to her?

Those who know her admire and respect her. They see her live out her Christianity twenty-four seven at work, at home, at church and at play. Some of her friends may even ask her about her faith and beliefs. They want to know her peace and secretly envy her convictions. They have questions. The entire world has questions for Christians. And Christians need to be ready with the answers.

In Acts 13 we read about an entire city that had questions for Paul and Barnabas. Antioch of Pisidia was filled with people who had eager hearts, desirous of learning more about God and His will for them—just like people today. Listen to these words:

> As Paul and Barnabas were going out, the people kept begging that these things might be spoken to them the

> next Sabbath. Now when the meeting of the synagogue had broken up, many of the Jews and of the God-fearing proselytes followed Paul and Barnabas, who, speaking to them, were urging them to continue in the grace of God. The next Sabbath nearly the whole city assembled to hear the word of the Lord (Acts 13:42–44).

What an amazing opportunity God gave Paul and Barnabas! Can you imagine nearly a whole city turning out just to hear more about God? Question: Do you think this powerful team showed up the next Sabbath to teach, to answer questions, and to help the cause of Christ? Or did they take the day off? Of course they showed up! Preaching the Good News of Jesus Christ was their entire reason for living! Paul and Barnabas lived to do the will of God. It was that simple.

The Holy Spirit inspired Peter to pen these words for the Christians in the first century and for the Christians today.

> But sanctify Christ as Lord in your hearts, always being ready to make a defense to everyone who asks you to give an account for the hope that is in you, yet with gentleness and reverence (1 Pet. 3:15).

"Always being ready" are solemn words for the Christian and must be taken seriously. God wants His children to be able to tell others why they believe what they believe and why they do what they do. And that takes commitment to the Word of God. And it takes sacrifice.

So let's add something to our day—a very necessary something: the Bible. Wake up; read your Bible; go to work; be nice. Let's not disappoint the Lord. Let's always be ready. Let's defend our faith. Let's get into the Word! Peter said it so rightly when he wrote: "But grow in the grace and knowledge of our Lord and Savior Jesus Christ" (2 Pet. 3:18).

It's time to study about a very important and intriguing woman who had tons of questions for the wisest man in the world.

CHAPTER

The Queen of Sheba: The Pearl Seeker

Scriptures: 1 Kings 10:1–13; 2 Chronicles 9:1–12

Song: "Wonderful Words of Life"

Imagine sitting at Solomon's feet and having the time to ask anything you wished and listening to profound answers from a very blessed king. The Queen of Sheba may have been royalty, but I sure do identify with her. Not her wealth, not her retinue, not her fame and fortune, but her desire to know more. How about you? What is outstanding to you in this woman who traveled so many miles to seek, to ask, to learn, and to understand from the wisest man alive at the time?

I cannot help but wonder about all the things she asked Solomon. I can only think of things I personally would love to have asked him. I also wonder what kind of relationship these two rulers had. I try to imagine their schoolroom and their animated discussions along with the mutual respect they seemed to have for one another.

Here is an intriguing kind of story. I want to know more about the Queen of Sheba. She traveled a long way because she wanted to learn. Now that's impressive. Let's see what God reveals about her.

TIME FOR A CLOSER LOOK

1. When did this event occur?

_____

_____

_____

2. Where did it take place?

_____

_____

_____

3. Where did the queen live?

_____

_____

_____

4. What was her purpose for visiting Solomon?

_____

_____

_____

5. What items are we told that she brought with her? What is a retinue?

_____

_____

_____

6. What does the Bible tell us about Solomon's attitude/behavior with her?

_____

_____

_____

7. Name the things that impressed the queen about Solomon's world.

_____

_____

_____

8. Fill in the blanks: "Behold, the _____ was not told me.
   . . . How blessed are your _____ who stand before you
   _____ and hear your _____" (1 Kings
   10:7–8).

9. Write out verse 9. What do you think about the Queen of Sheba's
   words here?

_____

_____

_____

10. What things did the queen give Solomon?

_____

_____

_____

11. What was Jesus saying in Luke 11:31? "The Queen of the South
    will rise up with the men of this generation at the judgment and
    condemn them, because she came from the ends of the earth to
    hear the wisdom of Solomon; and behold, something greater than
    Solomon is here."

_____

_____

_____

12. What would you have asked Solomon?

_____

_____

_____

13. How much do you want to learn about spiritual things?

_____

_____

_____

WHAT OTHERS HAVE SAID

Burton Coffman: This chapter appears to have been intended by the narrator to enhance in the fullest degree possible the glory and splendor of the reign of king Solomon. From an earthly viewpoint only did he succeed. Solomon's reign was a climax of sensuality and materialism. The gaudy ostentation of Solomon's court exhibits a false glitter, and, "One finds it easy to understand the judgment of Jesus Christ" (*The Layman's Bible Commentary,* Vol. 7, p. 42), who singled out the humble flowers of the meadow and declared that, "Even Solomon in all his glory was not arrayed like one of these" (Matt. 6:28–29).[1]

Adam Clarke: There was no more spirit in her.—She was overpowered with astonishment; she fainted. I have seen precisely the same effect produced; a lady who was herself an artist, viewing some exquisitely finished oriental paintings, was so struck with astonishment that she twice nearly fainted, and was obliged to leave the room. What happened to the queen of Sheba is a natural and not an uncommon effect which will be produced in a delicate sensible mind at the sight of rare and extraordinary productions of art.[2]

Matthew Henry: [The queen of Sheba came to Solomon] to hear his wisdom, thereby to improve her own (Matt. 12:42). . . . Our Saviour mentions her enquiries after God, by Solomon, as an aggravation of

---

1 Burton Coffman, *Coffman's Commentaries on the Bible,* 1 Kings 1:1, accessed Jan. 12, 2024. https://www.studylight.org/commentaries/eng/bcc/1-kings-10.html.

2 Adam Clarke, *Clarke's Commentary,* 1 Kings 10:5, accessed Jan. 12, 2024. https://www.studylight.org/commentaries/eng/acc/1-kings-10.html.

the stupidity of those who enquire not after God, by our Lord Jesus Christ.[3]

PRAYER

Our Father, thank You for loving us and blessing us with so many material blessings. Our hearts are full of love for You as we see our prayers answered and grow in Your Word. Thank You for Your faithfulness in staying by our side, even when we make so many mistakes. Thank You for Your grace in saving us. But most of all we thank You for Jesus. We thank You for Your marvelous Word that answers all our questions. Please don't give up on us. Please forgive us of our sins, Lord. May our hearts walk with your heart. Guide us, O Thou great Jehovah. In Jesus' name we pray, Amen.

---

3   Matthew Henry, *Henry's Complete Commentary on the Bible,* 1 Kings 10. https://www
    .studylight.org/commentaries/eng/mhm/1-kings-10.html.

A FINAL WORD

Well, did you learn anything? Did you see something or someone you had never encountered before? Keep on learning; keep on studying; and keep on loving God's precious Word. I am proud of you. Don't stop now.

—Becky

Therefore, if you have been raised up with Christ, keep seeking the things above, where Christ is, seated at the right hand of God. Set your mind on the things above, not on things that are on the earth. For you have died, and your life is hidden with Christ in God.

~Colossians 3:1–3

Printed in the USA
CPSIA information can be obtained
at www.ICGtesting.com
LVHW011521040624
782115LV00003B/11